THE FOURTH MESSENGER

The Fourth Messenger

A Musical

Book and Lyrics by
Tanya Shaffer

Music and Additional Lyrics by
Vienna Teng

Pictured on cover: Vienna Teng (seated) and Cailan Rose. Author photo by Cheshire Isaacs.

ISBN #: 978-0-692-54587-4

A Note from the Authors

      There's a fairy tale quality to the Buddha legend, with its terrain of prophecy, messengers, and quest. In re-imagining the Buddha as a contemporary woman, we sought to maintain the epic sweep of the story while simultaneously probing the essential human dilemma at its core. Is it possible, we asked, to be both enlightened and flawed? How do we reconcile contradictions within our heroes and within ourselves? Where do our responsibilities to ourselves, our loved ones, and the world begin and end? And how can we integrate the Buddha's guiding principle that attachment causes suffering with the intuitive notion that it is those very attachments that give meaning to our lives?

      The journey to this recording has been a long one. 2500 years since the Buddha's time, 15 years since the spark of the idea hit Tanya on a meditation retreat, 9 years since the two of us sat down in a San Francisco café to discuss the possibility of collaboration. Throughout this process, we've had to release our attachment to many things - melodies we loved, clever dialogue, poetic lyrics - to make room for the stronger narrative that lay beneath. Often the boundaries between playwright and composer, director and actor, have dissolved, as all of us tugged at the words, the plotlines, the melodies, the emotional arc of songs, until we felt them come alive. In artistic collaboration, the paradox of self and no-self is always present. When individual voices blend to form a new sound, that's where the magic happens.

i

Many wonderful artists have contributed to the creation of this piece. All of their spirits, and some of their voices, infuse this recording. We dedicate this project to them, and to the guy who inspired the story— Siddhartha Gautama, aka the Buddha, a human being who sought a pathway to happiness; a teacher who encouraged his students *not* to idolize him or follow blindly in his footsteps, but to test his ideas against their own direct experience and decide for themselves what is true.

The process of creating this musical has been a joyous one. It has changed our lives immeasurably. We hope it lives on in you.

-   Tanya Shaffer and Vienna Teng

The world premiere of *The Fourth Messenger* took place at the Ashby Stage in Berkeley, California, in February, 2013, with the following company:

Director: Matt August
Music Director: Christopher Winslow
Orchestrator: Robin Reynolds
Choreographer: Bridgette Loriaux
Set Design: Joe Ragey
Lighting Design: Steve Mannshardt
Costume Design: Fumiko Bielefeldt

CAST

MAMA SID	Annemaria Rajala
RAINA	Anna Ishida
ANDY	Jackson Davis
SUNNY	Will Springhorn Jr.
MAY	Alexis Wong
YASHA	Barnaby James
CLARA, HAG	Cathleen Riddley
DELILAH, DEREKH	Reggie D. White
MYRA	Bekka Fink
HARMONY, WATER	Simone Kertesz
MIKE, BREAD	Dave Garrett

The Fourth Messenger received developmental readings and workshops from Playwrights Foundation and TheatreWorks. Playwrights Foundation Artistic Director Amy Mueller was instrumental in the early development of the piece. Director Matt August played a key role in the later stages of development.

Cast of Characters

SID ARTHUR, aka MAMA SID, a world-renowned
spiritual teacher,
early 40's
RAINA, a reporting intern with Debunk Nation
magazine, early 20's
ANDY, Sid's assistant, 40's
SAM, Raina's editor, 40's or early 50's
BEV, a reporter with Debunk Nation, 40's or older
BILL, a reporter with Debunk Nation, 20's
JILL, a reporter with Debunk Nation, 20's
KEVIN, a reporter with Debunk Nation
CLARA, an Eastern European psychic
VLADIMIR, Clara's husband
SUNNY, Sid's father (in flashbacks), 30's or 40's
MAY, Sid's mother (in flashbacks), 30's
MYRA, a cancer patient and yogi (follower of Mama
Sid), 40's -
60's
MIKE, a businessman and yogi, 40's - 60's
DEREKH, with an "H" (pronounced like Derek without
an "h"), a   college student and yogi, early 20's
HARMONY, a former junkie and yogi, 20's
YASHA, Sid's high school boyfriend, 18
DELILAH, an emaciated, very ill drag queen
HAG, a very old woman
LOAF OF BREAD
GLASS OF WATER
POLICE OFFICER

ALSO BOIS RICHE COMMUNITY MEMBERS,
HOMELESS PEOPLE, ANGELS, PROTESTERS, POLICE
OFFICERS, REPORTERS

CASTING NOTE

"The Fourth Messenger" requires a minimum of 9
actors: 5 female and 4 male, with all except SID and
RAINA playing multiple roles. It can easily
accommodate a larger cast if desired.

iv

NOTES ON PUNCTUATION

A dash immediately following a word ("but -") indicates that the character has been interrupted, either by another character or by his/her own thought process.

Words in parenthesis right before a dash are the words the character is planning to say, which may trail off under the other character's line.

Three dots ("...") indicate a trailing off of the thought, rather than an abrupt interruption.

For the sake of flow and readability, we've chosen simply to note in the script when a song begins, rather than capitalizing or italicizing lyrics. Generally, when rhythmic line breaks occur the characters are singing, and when there are non-rhythmic interjections or the text reverts to prose, they are speaking. Within song lyrics, punctuation is kept to a minimum.

SONG LIST

ACT ONE

Overture (Instrumental)
Pebble in a Lake (Ensemble, Raina)
The Truth Must Come Out (Sam, Raina, Ensemble)
This Story is Mine (Raina, Sam)
Monkey Mind (Raina, Myra, Mike, Derekh, Harmony,
    Ensemble)
The Human Experience (Sid, Myra, Ensemble)
The Human Experience Reprise (Sid, Ensemble, Raina)
This Story is Mine Reprise (Raina)
Four Messengers Intro (Derekh, Harmony)
Four Messengers (Clara, May, Sunny, Vladimir, Derekh,
    Harmony)
Bois Riche (Derekh, Harmony, Sunny, Ensemble)
You've Got a Glow (Andy, Sid)
You've Got a Glow Tag (Andy)
Knock Knock (Raina, Sid)
Knock Knock Reprise (Sid, Andy)
Force of Nature (Sid, Raina)
The Real Thing (Ensemble, Delilah, Hag)

ACT TWO

Look to the Thought (Sid, Yasha, Ensemble)
I Will Not Rise (Sid, Ensemble)
Sid's Temptations
        Part 1: Bread and Water (Bread, Ensemble)
        Part 2: Sleep/Hundred Thousand Lifetimes
            (May, Sid, Ensemble)
        Part 3: Come Back to Me (Yasha, Sid, Ensemble)
It Was You (Sid)
What About Me? (Raina, Sid)
You Are There (Sid, Raina)
You've Got A Glow Reprise (Andy)
The Truth Must Come Out Reprise (Sam)
Aren't You Ashamed? (Ensemble)
This Story is Mine Final Reprise (Raina, Sid)
As Long as I Am Living (Sid, Raina, Ensemble)

Curtain Call Music: Look to the Thought Reprise
        (Sid, Raina, Ensemble)

vi

ACT 1, SCENE 1:

SONG: OVERTURE (INSTRUMENTAL)

As the house lights fade and the music rises, a large silhouette of MAMA SID, seated in the lotus position, is visible on a scrim. The image resembles the iconic outline of the Buddha seated in meditation. Lights go to almost black, then fade up on RAINA, the image on the scrim still dimly visible behind her. RAINA holds a book with an image of SID on the cover. She opens the book.

SONG: PEBBLE IN A LAKE

SID
Every choice that we make
Is a pebble in a lake
Spreading ripples beyond our sight.
Every step that we take
Impresses its shape
On a galaxy of lives

ENSEMBLE (OFFSTAGE)
Every choice that we make
Is a pebble in a lake
Spreading ripples beyond our sight
With every step that we take
Let the choices we make
Bring us closer to the light

(Spot focuses sharply on RAINA.)

RAINA
Every false move she's made
Every trust that she's betrayed
Left a wound that will never heal
Though she may think she's safe
Got away without a trace
One day all will be revealed

The past isn't gone
Its ghosts gather round
They live and they breathe

They hunger for answers.
The moment has come
To call you to account
And I will make my name
My breakout story will be your shame
For the truth will, the truth must come out.

SCENE 2

*The office of Debunk Nation magazine.   Reporters answer
phones, work at computers, make notes.*

SONG: THE TRUTH MUST COME OUT

REPORTERS
The truth, the truth, the truth will come out
The truth, the truth, the truth will come out
The truth, the truth, the truth will come out
The truth must come out

JILL
He said, she said

BILL
Fact check, follow up

REPORTERS
The truth must come out

BEV
I just have a few more questions

BILL
Fact check, follow up
Fact check, follow up
Fact check, follow up

BEV
The report from your department
Tells a different story

REPORTERS

A different story
A different story

SAM

Staff meeting!

REPORTERS

The truth, the truth, the truth, will come out
The truth, the truth, the truth, will come out
The truth, the truth, the truth, will come out
The truth, the truth, the truth, the truth-

(All move into place around a long table.)

SAM

The truth is we're in deep shit.

Subscriptions are shrinking
Ad rates are sinking
Our website's a stinking mess

Bloggers and tweeters
Are poaching our readers
In fifteen words or less!

We've gotta break something viral
To flip this downward spiral
Revitalize our dying base

We need a shock so volcanic
It spreads like a panic
From print to cyberspace

We need the next big story
Pitch it to me
The next big story

ALL

The next big story
What's it gonna be?

The next big story

SAM
We need Watergate, Wikileaks, Lewinsky scale
The holy grail of reporters' pay
Or you'll be writing Little League play-by-plays!
What's the next big story
Pitch it to me

SAM AND REPORTERS
What's the next big story?

RAINA
(Speaks) Mama Sid.

SAM
Raina! What are you doing back so soon?

BILL
Yeah, didn't your dad just die?

KEVIN
Jesus, Bill!

BEVERLY
Ever hear of tact?

SAM
We're glad you're back, Raina. *(Pointedly)* All of us. And
we're sorry for your loss.

(All murmur sympathy. They lack sincerity.)

RAINA
Thanks, Sam.

SAM
Sure. *(Slight pause.)* So...whatcha got?

RAINA
(Holds up book) An exposé of Mama Sid.

SAM

The guru?

BILL

The self-help lady?

BEV

The spiritual master?

RAINA

That's the one.

This "spiritual master"
Her name's grown faster
Than a hot tech start-up stock
You can't help but notice
The millions devoted
to her touchy-feely new age schlock
She's posing as the mother of the whole damn planet
Handing out answers and cures
One hundred percent pure
She's our next big story...

BEV

Honey, that's great, but if all you've got is a hunch...

(Reporters grumble their agreement with BEV.)

RAINA

Interviews are rare, no one dares to squeeze her
She keeps a tight grip on how the public sees her
Ask about her past, you get the Mona Lisa
Her private life: off-limits, please!

(All start tapping on their smartphones and computers)

KEVIN

She's on Wikipedia but needs citations

BEV

Nothing on Google but urban legends

BILL

Her mother was an elephant like Dumbo

JILL

No, her mother's lover was the jumbo

SAM

So her mythology's outsized
That's hardly a lead on a Pulitzer Prize

BILL

It was really sweet of you to give it a try
Ambitious intern

BEV

Sam, this might fly

RAINA

Have you ever seen a brick wall with nothing behind it?
No one puts a lock on an empty cabinet
Now we've got this guru keeping her silence
"Nothing to see here, folks"
I don't buy it
Someone's gonna scoop us sooner than later
Debunk nation ought to be the paper
To spill her scandalous secret
Just gotta find it, unwind it
And write the big bright headline
Of our next big story

BEV

We'd better act now
If we want the glory

ALL

The next big story

SAM

If we hunt it down

RAINA

We're talkin' big-time quarry

ALL

Nothing like a goddess falling down to earth
To strike a nerve with the masses
That's how we'll save our asses
With the next big story
The next big story
The next big story
The next big story
The next big story
The truth must come out.

SAM

Great. Let's do it.

RAINA

(Holding up a brochure) She's got a meditation center in Newfoundland *(Pronounced NU-fundlund)*. The winter retreat starts Monday.

SAM

Perfect. We'll send someone.

BILL AND JILL

I'll go. *(Look at each other.)* I'll go. *(Look at each other again)* I'll-

SAM

(Ignoring them) Bev, can you get there?

RAINA

What?

BEV

I'd have to cancel a few meetings, but sure.

RAINA

Wait –

SAM

(To Bev) Good, dress warm.

RAINA

No!

SAM

Thanks, everybody. Back to work.

(Staff disperses, except Sam and Raina.)

ALL (EXCEPT SAM AND RAINA)
(Singing softly) The truth, the truth, the truth, the truth
The truth, the truth, the truth, the truth...

> *(As soon as everyone is out of sight, SAM grabs RAINA in an embrace.)*

SAM

God, I missed you.

> *(They kiss, passionately. After a moment, RAINA pulls away.)*

RAINA

Sam.

SAM

Why didn't you call? I could've met you, I- (could've helped you out with some of the details)

RAINA

Sam!

SAM

What?

RAINA

(Fierce) I'm going. This was my idea.

SAM

Huh?

RAINA

My story. Mama Sid.

SAM

Oh. That. Well, honey-

RAINA

You promised me my own feature.

SAM

Well, yes, but... This lady's a master of spin. She'll be a very hard nut to crack. I need an experienced reporter.

RAINA

(Overlapping the word "reporter") I'm experienced! I've been here almost a year!

SAM

(Continuing over her interruption) Besides–

RAINA

Besides what?

SAM

You just got back! Your dad's funeral was just...It's too soon.

RAINA

You always say work is the best- (remedy for whatever is bothering you)

SAM

(Overlapping) I know, but... You're not ready.

SONG: THIS STORY IS MINE

RAINA

Not ready?

This story
It's got my name on it
There's no one else can do it right

SAM

Raina-

RAINA

I brought this
I've got a claim on it
I'm getting on that arctic flight

Good yogi I'll be
She'll gain trust in me
Then I'll strike

SAM

You know something about this lady?

RAINA

I know something
About hypocrisy
I know a lot about denial

I know something
About committing crimes
And never standing trial

One glance in her eyes
Unveils her disguise, and I know

This story is mine
I am all over it
There's no one else can do it justice

This story is mine

Sometimes you feel it so deep
You just have to trust it

So give up, give in, give me the green light
This is the story I was born to write.

(SAM looks at her for a long moment. Something in her
passion persuades him. He sighs.)

SAM

Okay.

RAINA

Yes! *(Kisses him passionately.)*

SAM

Just land it, okay? We wouldn't want anyone to think I
was playing favorites.

> *(SAM exits. As the set changes, RAINA appears in a*
> *spotlight. She pulls on her parka, picks up her*
> *suitcase, still holding the picture of MAMA SID.)*

RAINA

Just like that
In a single breath
Your entire life can change

A heartbeat stopped
A tether dropped
The whole world rearranged

There's truth to be told
And nothing to hold
Me back now

'Cause I know something
About duplicity
And something about loss

I know something

About blind ambition
And a lot about its cost

And oh, do I know anger
It's my old and trusty friend
Now it's time for me to learn
Something about revenge

This story
This story
This story is mine.

SCENE 3

*The meditation hall at SID's meditation center: an open space
with a small platform. On the platform is a cushion where
SID sits when giving her talks. During the transition, SID's
enlarged shadow/silhouette is again visible behind a scrim,
seated in the lotus position. Music comes in, YOGIS' voices
singing "in/out, in/out" as they enter the meditation hall,
carrying their cushions. SID's silhouette fades as the YOGIS
take their positions. An image of snow falling appears on the
scrim. RAINA sits on a cushion as well, slightly separated
from the others.*

SONG: MONKEY MIND

YOGIS

In, out, in, out
In, out, in, out
At last Relax
No more clutter, no more clatter
Time For mind
Tangle and chatter fade
Jungle is far away
Only breath, body, snow, silence
On this remote island
Remembering how to rest
Remembering how to breathe
Remembering how to be
Just be…

At peace…
Just me…

*(Chords continue for a few beats, then fade to
silence. Pause. RAINA fidgets.)*

RAINA

It's quiet
It is way too quiet
It's insanely quiet
I hear every little sound:
Bellies grumbling
Old pipes rumbling
Snowflakes tumbling all around!

Look at these nut cases. Sam would have a field day.
Sam. He wouldn't last ten sec-

ALL

Concentrate

RAINA

What will I say to her?
My first question?
Should I play the skeptic
Or the worshipper?
This is stupid.
Sitting freezing on the ground.
This is stupid.
Why does she make us wait around?
It's Just a power trip.
I'm getting out of here.
But I just got here!
What the hell is wrong with me?

It's like there's
Monkeys in my mind
Monkey mind
Monkeys in my mind
Monkey mind

Scolding and carping, my head's in a vice
Won't you shut up monkeys, won't you play nice?
Monkeys in my mind
Monkey mind
Monkey mind

Who is Mama Sid,
Guru beloved by all?
Will she look like her picture?
Will she be larger than life or small
Like the rest of us?

MYRA
I think I left the stove on.

ALL
Concentrate...

MYRA
Concentrate...
I just know I left the stove on!
Scrambled eggs, medium high
My house will burn down
My plants will all die
My photos, my clothes,
Everything I own
Everything I've saved
Damn it!

ALL
Concentrate...
Concentrate...

MIKE
"Small man in a big man's shoes"
How could my own brother say that to me?
"Small man in a big man's shoes"
In front of the entire family?

DEREKH
I'm not gonna think about my major

'Cause if I don't think about my major
The answer to what should be my major
Will just...come to me

HARMONY
Twelve months, six days, seven hours
Twelve months sober and clean
Twelve months, six days, seven hours
And five minutes
Yes!

MIKE
Did he pass the bar on the first try?
He's just jealous, of course that's why
I should feel compassion, I know
But I don't feel compassion, oh no,
I hate him!

ALL
Let go

MIKE
I hate him!

ALL
Let go
And love...

MIKE
But I can't!

ALL
But I can't
But I can't
It's like there's
Monkeys in my mind
Monkey mind
Monkeys in my mind
Monkey mind
Running and swinging and
Screaming and singing and

Laughing and talking and
Squeaking and squawking like
Monkeys in my mind
Monkey mind, monkey mind, monkey mind.

> *(While RAINA sings the following section, YOGIS
> rhythmically chant "In, out, in, out, in, out,
> concentrate")*

RAINA

Help!

I know cutthroat competition
I know the merciless routine
I know the headlong rush to deadline
Fueled by sugar and caffeine
But sitting so still
Makes me want to kill

I'm a city girl
Take me back to the city
Where the snow is black
And the air is gritty
Give me some familiar aggravation
Like shoving my way through a crowded train station
Give me noise and filth and degradation
Anything but this total deprivation
Of any stimulation at all!

Dad would have kept me from doing this
Oh Dad, I miss-

Shut up, shut up, shut up, shut up!

DEREKH

Economics, my dad says that's where the jobs are
Or engineering, safe bet there

HARMONY

Can I trust myself?
Can I love myself?

MYRA

If my house burns down, my homeowner's policy
Might be enough to cover my surgery

DEREKH

But all I want here is to be outside
Like a park ranger or a river raft guide

HARMONY

Can I face myself?
Embrace myself?

DEREKH

Don't think about that!
Don't think about that!

MYRA

But I shouldn't have to set my house on fire
To pay for surgery to keep me alive

MIKE

"Small man in a big man's shoes"
Is that what everybody else thinks too?

ALL

That's what everybody else thinks too!

MYRA

I'm gonna die!

ALL

I'm gonna die!

MYRA

I'm gonna die!

ALL

I'n gonna die!
I'm gonna die!
I'm gonna die!

I'm gonna die!

(All freeze. SID enters.)

SID
Kinda noisy in here, isn't it?

ALL
Monkeys in my mind
Monkey mind, monkey mind!

SID
(Smiles around the room) Friends. You've traveled a long way to get here. Your journey may have taken hours or days or even years. But you did it. You're here.

(Myra raises her hand.)

MYRA
(Words tumble out) I'm sorry, I have to go home. I think I left the stove on; I was making some eggs? I really wanted to come here, I've been planning it for so- but with the chemo, I've been so tired, and now I –

(SID puts a hand on her, interrupting the flow.)

MYRA (CONT'D)
(Breath. Softly) I'm so afraid.

SONG: THE HUMAN EXPERIENCE

SID
See the fear

MYRA
I see the fear

SID
What color is it?

18

MYRA

White.

SID

What shade?

MYRA

Blinding.

SID

Like sun on snow?

MYRA

Yes.

SID

Breathe through the fear

MYRA

Breathe through the fear
I'm trying to breathe through the fear
But how can I breathe through the fear?

SID

Feel the fear
Name the fear
It's just another
Texture here
Feel your Heart rate rising
The sweat appear
Part of the human experience

MYRA

Part of the human experience

SID

Now see the fear
The shape of the fear
Focus till it's crystal clear
You're outside of it now, peering in
At all of this human experience

MYRA

All of this human experience

(During the following, the lights open up, and SID begins to move among the yogis, including them each individually.)

SID

Now you are a painter
Noticing the light on the trees
now you are a scientist
Gazing through a microscope
You are a detective gathering clues
So keenly attuned
To everything around and inside you.
Joy

SID, DEREKH

And doubt

SID, MYRA, HARMONY

Fear

ALL EXCEPT RAINA

And rage
Feel them spark, ignite, and blaze
Let them burn themselves clean
And evaporate
Like all of this human experience

SID

Now see the grief
Name the grief

MEN

So tired of holding on so tight

SID

The act of naming brings relief

WOMEN
So tired of keeping up the fight

SID
Heavy, light, shallow, deep

ALL EXCEPT SID AND RAINA
Step outside your suffering

ALL EXCEPT RAINA
Part of the human experience

(SID returns to Myra.)

SID
See the fear
Feel the fear

MYRA
Hello, fear
I know you, fear
You're part of the human

SID
Part of the human

ALL
Part of the human experience.

(SID moves among the retreatants.)

SID
(To DEREKH) How's school?

DEREKH
Good, but...

SID
What to focus on?

DEREKH

Yeah.

SID

It'll come.

SID (CONT'D)
(To HARMONY) Thirteen months?

HARMONY

Almost!

SID

(To MIKE) City council?

MIKE

President this year.

SID
Wonderful. Let it in. *(To RAINA)* Sweetheart. It's wonderful to see you.

RAINA
(Stunned) Do you know me?

SID
That's a complex question.

RAINA
But... *(Attempting to recover herself)* Have we met?

SID
I don't think so. *(Sings)* Have we?

RAINA
(Sings) No. *(Breaks off. Speaks)* I mean... No. We haven't.

SID
Oh, I'm sorry. *(Curtsies, mock serious.)* I am Sid.

RAINA

Yes, I know; I am Peace.

SID

Peace. *(Considering.)* Mm. Peace. *(Looks at her closely.)*
Are you sure that we haven't met before?

RAINA

Nope.

SID

Not in this present lifetime?

(RAINA shakes her head.)

SID (CONT'D)

Just kindred spirits then, I guess.

RAINA

Guess so.

*(SID looks at her closely for another moment.
RAINA shifts uncomfortably.)*

SID

So how's the meditation going?

RAINA

Fine.

SID

Really? Fine? You don't feel like commandeering the
truck and hightailing it out of this frozen hellhole?

RAINA

(Stares) I...

SID

Don't worry. Everyone feels that way on their first
retreat.

RAINA

Is it that obvious?

SID

Yes, it is.

RAINA

What, do I have "Novice" tattooed on my forehead in green ink?

SID

Yes, you do, but it suits you. Green's your color. *(Smiles)* So why do we do it, this meditation thing?

(Derekh and Harmony's hands shoot up.)

DEREKH

Oo! Oo! *(SID nods at him.)* To clear our minds.

MIKE

To focus our minds.

HARMONY

To get all quiet and peaceful inside.

SID

Peace?

RAINA

You tell me. You're the teacher.

SID

I am? I thought you were!

RAINA

I...I don't...

SID

I'm sorry. You're right. For the purposes of this moment, I am "The Teacher." But instead of a class, let's think of this as a workshop. And instead of asking, "Why are we sitting here?" let's ask, "What are we building?"

So everybody close your eyes for a moment. And now imagine, with each breath...

SONG: THE HUMAN EXPERIENCE REPRISE

SID (CONT'D)

You're building a container
Picture an enormous wooden bowl
Building a container
And there's nothing it can't hold
A vessel deep and wide
To hold all of your life
You're building a container called awareness

> (RAINA frowns slightly. SID puts a hand on
> her shoulder. RAINA flinches, then settles into
> it. Yogis harmonize underneath the following
> section.)

SID (CONT'D)

So whatever you are feeling
However subtle or intense
A part of you is larger
Than even the darkest circumstance
The ocean holds the waves
The fire holds the flames

SID AND YOGIS

And you can hold it all
In your awareness...

SID

Welcome to the winter retreat.

> (SID watches RAINA for a moment. "The Human
> Experience" theme continues as the lights and scene
> shifts. SID exits.)

RAINA

(Softly) Hello, grief.

(Her eyes fly open. She looks around.)

RAINA (CONT'D)

Oh no. No. Damn. Damn, damn, damn, damn damn!

SONG: THIS STORY IS MINE REPRISE

RAINA (CONT'D)

Something about the way you work
Really gets under the skin
If I don't cling tight to what I know
Even I could be taken in
I'd lay down my arms
Fall for your charms
And be lost...

But that's not how this story goes
'Cause I'm not such easy prey
The next time we come face to face
I'll be prepared to play
I'll be your new best friend
The one you can trust in
Until in the end
You'll confess to me

This story
This story
This story is mine

SCENE 4

RAINA crosses, talking on her cell phone. She checks frequently to make sure no one is near. In another part of the stage, SAM talks on the phone in his office. Sam's last name is pronounced "SAH-ra."

SAM

Debunk Nation, Sam Sara speaking.

RAINA

She's good, Sammy.

SAM

Well, hello to you too.

RAINA

She's tricky. She plays on your emotions.

SAM

Who?

RAINA

Who.

SAM

Oh. Well, sure. You don't become the world's "leading spiritual teacher" if you can't move product. What did you expect?

RAINA

I don't know. Not this. *(Her voice catches slightly.)*

SAM

Hey...You okay?

RAINA

I'm fine. It's just...

SAM

Getting cold feet?

RAINA

No! I mean, literally, yeah, this place is stuck in the goddamn ice age, but I'm not-

SAM

How can I help?

RAINA

Ah, some body heat, maybe?

SAM

Generating it as we speak.

RAINA

Could you Fed Ex it? Because I could use a
little...human...

SAM

Sweetie, you can do this. Don't get bogged down. Just
take the... juice... from whatever it is you're going
through - grieving your dad, missing me, all of that -
and put it right back into the work. That's what makes
you such a fierce little-

RAINA

I know all that! Why are you –

SAM

Easy. I'm just concerned about you, that's all.

RAINA

You mean you're concerned about your story.

SAM

Your story. And yes. I'm concerned about both.

RAINA

Look, everything's fine, okay? We're right on schedule.
I've already connected with Mama Sid once, and we're
having a private chat later today. I think she's kind
of...drawn to me.

SAM

How could she help herself?

(Bev pokes her head in.)

BEV

Sam, your wife's on line two.

SAM

(Gesturing to BEV that he'll be right there. To RAINA)
Listen, I've gotta go. Call again soon, okay?

SCENE 5

The kitchen. HARMONY is peeling potatoes. DEREKH is chopping onions. They are intensely focused. RAINA enters, holding a recipe.

RAINA

3 cups black, 3 cups pinto, 3 cups kidney. What are we making again?

DEREKH

Three-bean soup.

RAINA

Didn't we have that for lunch?

DEREKH

That was two bean.

(Harmony's peel breaks.)

HARMONY

I don't think we're supposed to be talking.

RAINA AND DEREKH

Sorry.

(Derekh continues chopping. RAINA studies the recipe.)

HARMONY

I'm not trying to be a pill. It's just - I'm kind of an all or nothing person. So if I start talking... But you guys go ahead. I just won't participate.

DEREKH

That's cool.

RAINA

(To Derekh, softly.) What was your name again?

DEREKH

Derekh. With an "h." (RAINA gives him a perplexed look.) It's silent. (Raina nods, still confused.) Yours?

RAINA

Peace.

HARMONY

Peace? Oh, that's so funny! I'm Harmony!

RAINA

What a coincidence!

HARMONY

Yeah, right? I mean, what are the chances? *(Catching herself)* Oh gosh, see what I mean? Once I start I can't stop! *(She zips her mouth, goes back to peeling.)*

RAINA

(To DEREKH) So...how long have you been a follower of Mama Sid?

HARMONY

Isn't she amazing? I never could have gotten clean without her. Before I met her, I didn't know what to do with this pain inside me. I wanted to be someone else. I'd claw at my skin, and pound on my belly...

DEREKH

Heavy.

HARMONY

But Mama Sid... She sees me, you know? And what she sees is good, and pure, and true. And seeing her see me, I start to see myself that way too, see?

RAINA

I see.

DEREKH

I feel you. I-

HARMONY

Why are you here, Peace? It doesn't seem like you're really... I don't know...

RAINA

Oh, well, see, I used to do yoga, and some Sufi dancing, but then—

DEREKH

I knew it! *(To HARMONY)* She's a hopper.

RAINA

A hopper?

DEREKH

You know, you hop from one spiritual practice to another, looking for the one that smokes your salmon. That's cool. That's what Mama Sid did before she found her own way.

She and Andy, her helper dude, lived in, like, fifteen different communities. Hare Krishna, Moonies, Mormons, even, like, Orthodox Jews, with the little ringlets and stuff. *(Illustrates with his hands)*.

RAINA

But where was she before that? No one seems to know anything about her.

DEREKH

We know all kinds of stuff.

RAINA

How? There's nothing on the-

DEREKH

You're looking in the wrong place. What you need to
know isn't out there. It's in here.

RAINA

But –

HARMONY

We know about the prophecy.

DEREKH

You've heard of the prophecy, right? The four
messengers?

RAINA

The elephant, right? Something about an elephant?

HARMONY

(Giggling, excited) I don't think she knows.

RAINA

Well, everybody's got a different version.

DEREKH

Here's the story, morning glory. It started out like any
other night.

SONG: FOUR MESSENGERS INTRO

DEREKH (CONT'D)

While Mama Sid's own mama
Lay sleeping in her bed,
Her husband sawing logs beside her,
Like he always did...

Into her dream there burst a stranger
An elephant as white as the foaming sea
She tried to scream; no sound escaped her
The elephant dropped gently onto its knee
Then From its trunk it pulled out a flower
She swooned to feel its heat and its power

IT drew her close and they danced intimately!

HARMONY
(Giggling) Very intimately.

DEREKH
Then all at once, the elephant,
It disappeared into her side!

HARMONY
Then came a knock upon the door
Right In the middle of the night...

SCENE 6

*Lights come up on MAY and SUNNY's house. A doorbell is
heard, then the sound of someone banging.*

CLARA
(Offstage) Misses Arthur! Mister Arthur! Open up!

> *(MAY rushes out, tying the belt on her robe. She has
> just gotten up. She opens the door. CLARA, an
> Eastern European psychic, bursts in. She is dressed
> in flowing gypsy garments.)*

MAY
Clara! What are you doing here?

CLARA
I felt it. I felt it.

> *(CLARA's husband VLADIMIR rushes in behind
> her, humming, hands outstretched. DEREKH and
> HARMONY transform themselves into her son and
> daughter and join him.)*

MAY
(Looking at VLADIMIR, DEREKH, and HARMONY) Who
are they?!

CLARA

It was here... No wait, it was here... *(She rushes around the room, hands outstretched to feel the vibrations. Her husband and son follow. She extends her hands toward the bedroom.)* No...Right here!

> *(SUNNY explodes out from the bedroom, toting a baseball bat.)*

SUNNY

What the hoo-ha is going on out here??! *(Seeing Clara)* You?! *(To MAY)* May, tell me you didn't schedule a palm reading at two in the morning! *(MAY shakes her head. To the men)* And who the hell are these people?

VLADIMIR

Vladimir Alexandrovich Voronov.

DEREKH

Peter Vladimirovich Voronov.

HARMONY

Anastacia Vladimirovna Voronov Finklestein.

SUNNY

Who?

VLADIMIR

Her husband.

DEREKH

Her son.

HARMONY

Her daughter.

VLADIMIR, DEREKH, HARMONY

(With a flourish) Ha!

SUNNY

I knew this fortune-telling hokum was getting out of hand!

(Clara goes into a kind of trance)

CLARA

Oooooooooooh! Oooooooooooh!

(VLADIMIR, DEREKH, and HARMONY babble excitedly in a fake Slavic language.)

MAY

Clara? Are you all right?

(Clara's eyes snap open)

SONG: FOUR MESSENGERS

CLARA

The elephant came to you, is it true?

MAY

What?

CLARA

The white elephant came to you, is this true?

MAY

Well, yes, that is, I did dream of an elephant, but–

CLARA

I knew it!

(VLADIMIR, DEREKH, and HARMONY cheer and embrace.)

CLARA (CONT'D)

The ancient prophets all foretold it

DEREKH, HARMONY, VLADIMIR
Ha!

CLARA
The pachyderm now bears it out

DEREKH, HARMONY, VLADIMIR
Ha!

CLARA
The long-awaited day is finally here

DEREKH, HARMONY, VLADIMIR
Oompah, oompah, oompah, oompah
Oompah, oompah, oompah, oompah

MAY
I'm sorry, I don't follow you.

CLARA
With his immense well-formed proboscis

DEREKH, HARMONY, VLADIMIR
Ha!

CLARA
The giant mammal plants the seed

DEREKH, HARMONY, VLADIMIR
Ha!

CLARA
For a flower which has no earthly peer

DEREKH, HARMONY, VLADIMIR
Oompah, oompah, oompah, oompah
Oompah, oompah, oompah, oompah

SUNNY
Come again?

CLARA
Within your womb the seed is growing

DEREKH, HARMONY, VLADIMIR
Ha!

MAY
What?!

CLARA
A couple months and she'll be showing

DEREKH, HARMONY, VLADIMIR
Ha!

SUNNY AND MAY
Huh?

CLARA
What part of "you're knocked up" isn't crystal clear?

MAY AND SUNNY
We're pregnant!

> *(MAY and SUNNY embrace. VLADIMIR and DEREKH slap SUNNY on the back, congratulating him in their language.)*

CLARA
And this is not just any baby, oh no. A being such as this comes but once in ten thousand years! A being so noble, so majestic, that even the birds and the beasts bow down to pay their respects!

> *(VLADIMIR and DEREKH again slap SUNNY on the back, shouting further congratulations.)*

SUNNY
Yeah? What's he gonna be? A captain of industry like his papa?

CLARA
The possibilities are boundless
So many paths that fate could take
But you can trust in a life beyond compare

MAY

How exciting!

SUNNY

A general...

MAY
Commanding troops on land and water

SUNNY

A president...

MAY
Creating law with the wave of a hand
A movie star...

SUNNY

the world's first

SUNNY & MAY

Trillionaire

MAY
A super-athlete - top of the game

SUNNY
A power broker, a money machine

MAY, SUNNY
Greater than the world's ever seen...

CLARA
All of that is possible, yes. But there is another option:

A noble teacher your child could be
A kind of tour guide to the mysteries
Renouncing the materialist class
To pursue the spirit's path
Holy mendicant roaming the land
Spreading wisdom and joy with the touch of a hand

MAY

Oh, my!

SUNNY

(Alarmed) Holy...mendicant?! A beggar, you mean?

CLARA

Only in the most trivial sense!

SUNNY

So my kid will either be rich and powerful or some kind
of homeless wacko?!

CLARA

I never said-

SUNNY (CONT'D)

What's gonna make the difference? What's gonna tilt the
scales between option number one and option number
two?

CLARA

Well, since you ask...

> *(Closes her eyes, enters a trancelike state.*
> *VLADIMIR, DEREKH, and HARMONY join her.)*

CLARA, VLADIMIR, DEREKH, HARMONY
Hmmmmmmmmmm....

CLARA

If the child is to become the awakened one, the holy
mendicant, the great wandering sage...

(She opens her eyes.)

CLARA (CONT'D)

Four messengers
Four messengers
Will be the storm
That bursts the dam

ALL

Four messengers
Four messengers

SUNNY

Could do much harm
I need a plan!

So who are they? What do they look like? What are their names?

CLARA

Messengers numbers one, two and three
Ambassadors of life's fragility
Harbingers of every creature's plight:
Existence is both harsh and fleeting
All that's strong shall one day weaken
We are born to sicken, age and die

SUNNY

So these first three messengers who will transform my kid into a... spiritual peddler... will be icons of sickness, aging, and death?

CLARA

You could put it that way.

SUNNY

What about the fourth messenger?

CLARA

The fourth. Ah...the fourth.
A grain of hope, a hint of light

A spark of possibility...

SUNNY
So that's grain, hint or spark?

CLARA
A glimmer that this earth just might
Hold more than what the eyes can see
With a pure and shining presence
This messenger inspires a dream
Of a pathway to transcendence
A path to set all creatures free
Once your child has seen this vision
No force on earth can stem the tide
Compassion streaming into wisdom
Spurring on your noble child

CLARA, VLADIMIR, DEREKH, HARMONY
Four messengers
Four messengers
Will point the way
To what's beyond

Four messengers
Four messengers
Will spur this
Young soul to become

VLADIMIR
The teacher,

DEREKH
The prophet

HARMONY
The seer

CLARA
The sage,
The one who shines light on this desolate age

The one whose compassion is vaster than earth

ALL
Who unlocks the secrets of death and rebirth -

MAY
Death and rebirth!

SUNNY
No way in hell!

CLARA
You don't have to yell.

SUNNY
Sickness, aging, death, and some holy freak
These are the four my kid's never gonna see
Then he'll grow up to be a tycoon like me!
I will surround him with young, healthy people
I'll build a fortress, the walls will be stout
and I will keep those four damn messengers out!

*(Lights shift back to RAINA, DEREKH, AND
HARMONY chopping vegetables.)*

DEREKH
That dude was so freaked out thinking his kid was
gonna see those messengers - sickness, old age, death,
and a...like a...

HARMONY
An awakened soul.

DEREKH
Right. He was so terrified that she'd see those things and
end up on the streets –

HARMONY
He built her a town to keep them out.

RAINA

A town?

HARMONY

He was a very powerful man. The place had some Frenchy French name, like La Belle Plage or Le Pain Quotidien, something like that.

SONG: BOIS RICHE

SUNNY

It's actually called Bois Riche.

HARMONY

Right. It was like a walled city. Totally self-contained. He invited some of his high-powered business friends to come live there, and then the word spread.

> *(Citizens of Bois Riche begin walking on, carrying store fronts, trees, flowers, etc. They are all dressed in athletic clothes, tanned and fit and smiling.)*

SUNNY

It's another lovely day in
Bois Riche, Bois Riche!
Bois Riche, Bois Riche!

HARMONY

Sun is shining, flowers blooming

DEREKH

Brooks are burbling, children singing,

COMMUNITY MEMBERS

The ice cream truck jingles down the street

SUNNY
(Confidentially) It's actually nonfat yoghurt with
sucralean - the kids don't know the difference!
Childhood obesity is a problem you won't find here.

COMMUNITY MEMBERS
Everything is ideally proportioned in
Bois Riche, Bois Riche!
Bois Riche, Bois Riche!
Nothing unlovely troubles the eye
From the soft green grass to the clear blue sky
Bois Riche, Bois Riche!

RAINA
What does Bois Riche mean, anyway?

DEREKH
"Rich wood," I think.

RAINA
And this town is where?

DEREKH
Search me.

(RAINA looks at HARMONY, who also shrugs.)

HARMONY
You had to have money to live there

MEN
We say that without any shame

DEREKH
Dozens applied and got turned aside

COMMUNITY MEMBERS
Though we sympathize, we're not to blame

WOMEN
We're wealthy because we are worthy

MEN
We've all worked so very hard

OLDER COMMUNITY MEMBERS
Or our parents did for us

YOUNGER COMMUNITY MEMBERS
Or their parents did for them

COMMUNITY MEMBERS
Well let's not pursue the matter too far...

HARMONY AND DEREKH
Everyone is beautiful in
Bois Riche, Bois Riche!
Bois Riche, Bois Riche!

MEN
Our bodies toned, we're Olympically fit

WOMEN
All that nature has denied us
plastic surgeons can fix

ALL
Oh ugliness is something that we will not abide
It starts skin deep but then it rots you inside
If you're looking for substance let style be your guide
In Bois Riche!

(Focus shifts to SUNNY.)

SUNNY
(To HARMONY, DEREKH, and RAINA) Thinking of
buying in? Come on out here, Sidney! This is my little
girl. Shall we tell these good people about a few of the
amenities we have to offer?

SID
You bet!

SUNNY

Botanical gardens

SID

Our own private zoo

SUNNY

Movies and concerts

SID

And theatre too!

SUNNY
Every type of cuisine you could possibly wish

SUNNY AND SID

Stables
An ice rink

SUNNY
a pond stocked with fish
Saunas and steam rooms, infinity pools
State-of-the-art gyms and outstanding schools
Synagogues, Churches, boutiques and a mall
Professional golf course, oh we've got it all

Would you like an application?

(Pulls out a tome the size of a phone book.)

It's a little thick, for security reasons. For the sake of the
children, you understand.

Our children these precious creatures
Full of innocence, purity, joy
I can't bear the mere thought of their
Fragile little psyches destroyed by

ALL
Violence, hatred poverty crime

SUNNY

We'll keep these far away from their minds.

WOMAN 1

Children grow up someday

ALL

But ours won't if we fulfill our design.

SUNNY

Here, children can be children, into adulthood and beyond!

ALL

So lock that gate and let the riffraff choke
Inside paradise we're full of hope
And nothing unlovely troubles the eye
From the soft green grass to the clear blue sky
Bois Riche, Bois Riche
Bois Riche, Bois Riche
Bois Riche, Bois Riche
Bois Riche!

> *(Citizens of Bois Riche exit. Focus returns to the kitchen.)*

RAINA

Mama Sid just went from one cut-off, sheltered community to another.

DEREKH

What do you mean?

RAINA

She grew up in her daddy's little glassed-in world, then she came up here and built her own.

HARMONY

But it's totally different!

RAINA

How so?

HARMONY

Her dad was trying to deny reality. Mama Sid helps people embrace it.

DEREKH

Yeah.

RAINA

Then why does she have to come out in the middle of nowhere to do it? Why not do it in New York City?

HARMONY

She goes to New York, she goes to Calcutta, she goes everywhere!

RAINA

But this is the home she's created. Clearly there's something she's trying to shut out.

DEREKH

(Giggling) Whoa, seriously? You're, like, psychoanalyzing Mama Sid?

HARMONY

Wow, Peace, you're really carrying around a lot of distrust. Do you have a good relationship with your mother?

RAINA

(Ignoring this) And how do you even know all this stuff anyway?

DEREKH

Dude, you gotta quit asking that. I told you: everyone knows. Uh oh, here comes Andy. We better get this shit cooked.

> *(They go quickly back to chopping as ANDY walks by. Lights fade.)*

SCENE 7

*Outside the meditation hall. RAINA and ANDY shovel
snow.*

ANDY
Of course they're all just stories. Only Sidney knows
what really happened.

RAINA
But where do the stories come from?

ANDY
Search me. *(Slight pause. They continue shoveling.)* Lotta
powder today.

RAINA
Yep. *(Playful, slightly flirtatious)* So Andy... What exactly
is your relationship to Mama Sid?

ANDY
My "relationship" to her?

RAINA
Uh huh.

ANDY
Well... She's my teacher, my colleague, my boss, and my
dearest friend.

RAINA
Is that all?

ANDY
Isn't that enough?

RAINA
(Suggestive) Is it?

ANDY

You're a tricky one, aren't you?

RAINA

Haven't you ever wanted more from her?

ANDY

Have I ever wanted more? Sure, I'll cop to that.
Twenty- some years ago, when I met Sidney, I was a
nineteen-year-old pipsqueak who didn't have a clue
what to do with his life. That kind of desire - the
physical kind - was the only kind I could put a name to.

RAINA

Where'd you guys meet?

ANDY

The Squalid Squat, we called it, or, in more illustrious
moods, the Temple of Corporeal Transcendence. It's a
familiar scene: we thought we were spiritual pioneers,
pushing the frontiers of consciousness, when really we
were a bunch of confused kids taking all the drugs we
could get our hands on and eating out of dumpsters. I
found Sid curled up in a doorway - she hadn't eaten in
days - and persuaded her to come home with me. For
weeks, I tried every trick in the book to get her into bed.

RAINA

No luck?

ANDY

Nah. Sid was never interested in that.

RAINA

Never?

ANDY

Nope, never. Not with me, not with anyone. She's a... a
pure spirit. In the world but not of it. Then one night I
woke up and she was packing her bags.

*(Lights illuminate the squat. SID is packing.
ANDY crosses to his sleeping bag, sits up as if just
woken. They speak softly so as not to wake the
others.)*

ANDY

What are you doing?

SID

Leaving.

ANDY

Why?

SID

It's not here.

ANDY

What?

SID

What I'm looking for.

ANDY

Where will you go?

SID

I don't know.

SONG: YOU'VE GOT A GLOW

ANDY
(Pause) Take me with you.

SID

Why?

ANDY

You've got something.

51

SID

(Laughs) Like...the flu, maybe?

ANDY

I'm serious!

SID

I'm sorry. I'll miss you too.

ANDY

I need you.

SID

Andy.

ANDY

You've got something I can't name.

SID

We've been through this. It's nothing personal. I'm just
not interested in that kind of relationship.

ANDY

That's not what I mean.

You've got a glow
You shine like the sun
I want to be near you
And I'm not the only one
We're drawn to your orbit
Reflect back your light
So let me come with you
Don't walk out alone into the night

SID

Andy, all of that is just what you're projecting onto me.

ANDY

No. It's more than that.

You've got a glow

You awaken my mind
The moment you enter
The room just comes alive
It's not infatuation
It's Deeper than desire
So please take me with you
Don't walk out alone into the fire

SID

I'm just a pilgrim
The glow that you see
Is simply your own burning
Need to arise and be free
I've nothing to show you
No magical spark
So I can't take you with me
When I walk alone into the dark

My hands are empty of gifts
I'm still trying to learn how to live

ANDY

Let me follow you, Sid

SID

Andy I've nothing to teach
There's no wisdom to in following me

ANDY

Then at least
Let me walk beside you
That's all that I ask
Let me shoulder some weight
In this daunting task
We share the same dream
A dream that will grow
Sidney, dear Sidney
You know more than you know...
You've got a glow

SID

No more than your own

ANDY

You shine like the sun

SID

So does everyone

ANDY

I'm seeking the answers

SID & ANDY

And I'm not the only one
I'm drawn into orbit
Propelled into flight
Compelled to keep searching
Until I emerge into the light

ANDY

So please take me with you
Don't walk out alone into the night

(Focus shifts back to RAINA and ANDY.)

RAINA

So you became her disciple instead of her lover.

ANDY

And I've never had a moment's regret.

RAINA

Did she ever tell you why she left home in the first place?

ANDY

Nope.

RAINA

I mean, whether something happened there, that-

ANDY
Sid doesn't talk about the past.

RAINA
Doesn't that bother you?

ANDY
She's entitled to her privacy, same as anyone else.

RAINA
But after all these years that you two have been friends...

ANDY
(Slightly edgy) I let her know years ago that if there's
ever anything she wants to talk about, I'm here for her.
And if she doesn't, that's her prerogative.

RAINA
But don't you think-

ANDY
Peace, why are you asking me this? If there's something
you want to know about Sidney, she's the one you
should be asking.

RAINA
I'm just curious, that's all. I'd never ask you to betray her
trust.

ANDY
(Looks at her strangely) Of course not. Now go sweep the
front step. Please.

(RAINA exits.)

SONG: YOU'VE GOT A GLOW TAG

ANDY (CONT'D)
The privilege to walk beside you
Is all I've ever asked

Just to shoulder some weight in your daunting task
To share in the dream
To bask in your glow
Sidney, dear Sidney, it means more than you know...

SCENE 8

Outside the meditation hall.

HARMONY
He's married?

MIKE
Who?

RAINA
Nobody.

HARMONY
Her boyfriend.

MIKE
Oh boy.

HARMONY
And he's her boss.

RAINA
Harmony!

HARMONY
We're all friends here, Peace.

MYRA
Yeah. *(Eyeing MIKE)* We're not here to judge.

MIKE
Right, we're just a bunch of supportive, empty-headed ladies.

MYRA

What is your problem?

MIKE
You think encouraging her to sleep with her married boss is being a friend?

MYRA
I think you really need to work on those anger issues, mister city council bigshot.

HARMONY
Yeah.

MIKE
"Messy attachment," Mama Sid calls it. *(To MYRA)* Or don't you listen to her either?

MYRA
Ignore him.

MIKE
How old is this guy, anyway?

RAINA
They're separated, kind of.

MIKE
Kind of?

RAINA
They live together, but they don't sleep together. It's -

MIKE
Please don't say "complicated."

RAINA
- a difficult situation.

HARMONY
Do you love him?

RAINA

We don't really use that word, but... He's great - he's funny, and smart, and-

MIKE

Smart enough to have his cake and-

MYRA

(To MIKE) Hush. *(To Raina, sympathetically)* You deserve better.

MIKE

That's what I said!

RAINA

(Lightly) Come on. You guys barely know me. Maybe I deserve exactly what I've got.

HARMONY

That's what I used to think of myself too, before Mama Sid showed me my true face. Don't worry. She'll show you yours too.

(DEREKH enters.)

DEREKH

I figured it out.

MYRA

What?

DEREKH

I'll do a triple major. Engineering, environmental studies, art history, and phys ed.

MIKE

That's four.

DEREKH

Shit!

(DEREKH, MIKE, HARMONY, and MYRA exit.)

SCENE 9

Lights shift to SID's office. SID and RAINA are laughing.
SID is laughing so hard she's falling over.

SID

Stop!

RAINA

I'm serious! You've got to change up the diet around here. Either that or provide gas masks. I mean, the hall's big, but it's not that big. And with the windows closed and the heater on... whew!

SID

(Still laughing) Okay, okay. I'll talk to Andy about it.

RAINA

Hasn't anybody mentioned this before?

SID

Nobody.

RAINA

And you've never noticed.

SID

I'm afraid not.

RAINA

So much for awareness.

SID

(Laughs) Peace, you are a card. You should be a comedian.

RAINA

You just don't get out much.

SID

I guess not. I haven't laughed like this in...I don't know.

RAINA

It must be hard.

SID

What?

RAINA

Being cut off from regular people. Always having to be "on."

SID

(Laughs) Oh, it's not –

RAINA

I mean, what were you like before?

SID

Before what?

RAINA

Before you were, you know, "Mama Sid."

SID

Before I was Mama Sid, I was just Sid.

RAINA

Who is Sid?

SID

Who is Peace?

RAINA

I asked you first.

SID

Knock knock

RAINA

Who's there?

(SID says nothing.)

RAINA (CONT'D)

What? What? Oh, I get it. There's nobody there. You're nobody. (SID touches her nose.) Come on. You're a world-famous guru!

SID

Guru schmuru.

RAINA

(Overlapping) You have millions of followers.

SID

The *teachings* have followers.

RAINA

You created the teachings.

SID

No. I created nothing. I just stumbled around in the dark until I tripped over them.

RAINA

So that's it? That's why you won't talk about yourself? Because you're "nobody"?

SID

Because it's irrelevant. I had an experience that transformed me, and now that experience speaks through me. Nothing else matters.

RAINA

Oh, but it does.

SONG: KNOCK KNOCK

RAINA (CONT'D)
Knock knock

SID
Who's there?

RAINA
Someone who wants to know you
The you when you were younger, still becoming
Knock knock

SID
Who's there?

RAINA
Someone who needs the whole truth
Someone who wants to know the steps and stumbling
Your students open up
And reveal themselves to you
If you would do the same,
We could see you're human too
And start to feel we also can break through!

SID
Knock knock

RAINA
Who's there?

SID
The welcome mat is empty
The clamor in your ears is your soul calling
Knock knock

RAINA
Who's there?

SID

I know it can be tempting
But focusing outside yourself, you're stalling
The road map of our suffering
leads right back to ourselves
There's nothing to be gained
Imitating someone else
I offer you a compass
But my path isn't yours
You've got to open up your own doors

RAINA

I see.

SID

You see?

RAINA

Oh sure.
Knock knock

SID

Who's there?

RAINA

Now everything is clearer
How carefully you craft these lessons for us
Knock knock

SID

Who's there?

RAINA

You're holding up a mirror
For us to understand ourselves—how generous!
And how convenient that you're standing
Behind the one-way glass
A teacher never shows
Any weakness to her class
Or if she ever screwed up
Somewhere in her past...

Now you are a guru
Though of course you never use the name
Now you are a hero
Even as you seem to shun your fame
Rise high above the rest
No secrets to confess
You're building the mystique of the
Beautiful, flawless, untarnished
And wise Mama Sid
It's a brilliant story
A brilliant story-

SID

Peace.

RAINA

Hm?

SID

Why are you here?
What is it that you yearn for?
I'd like to understand what drives your anger

RAINA

Knock knock

SID

Who's there?

RAINA

I'm doing you a favor
I'm giving you a chance to live with candor

SID AND RAINA

You're clinging tight to something
That's bringing you to grief
Until you can release it,
You'll never find relief
And don't you know the truth will set you free?

RAINA

Knock knock

SID

Who's there?
Knock knock

RAINA

Who's there?

SID AND RAINA

Knock knock
Knock knock.

SCENE 10

SID crosses to her desk. ANDY is also in the office, at his computer.

ANDY

Knock knock? Earth to Sidney, come in, Sidney.

SID

Huh?

ANDY

I said, we've got you at the Spring Retreat in Assisi May 5-12, then back in Paris at the Sorbonne May 14 –

SID

Fine.

ANDY

But... you're due at the Himalayan Retreat the morning of May 16, and with the road conditions there, I don't see how you'd make it.

SID

Okay.

ANDY

The Himalayan one's been set for a while, and the
Sorbonne can probably reschedule, so maybe we should-

SID

(Snaps) Just work it out, okay?

ANDY

(Shocked) Sidney?

SID

I'm sorry. *(Pause)* I'm sorry, Andy. I didn't mean to... It's
just...

ANDY

What?

SID

It's her.

ANDY

Who?

SID

That girl. Peace.

ANDY

Oh. Piece of work, is more like it.

SID

Andy! Meow.

ANDY

She's...sneaky. I don't like it.

SID

She wants...something.

ANDY

Don't they all?

SID

A want so great as to be a need.

ANDY

What does she want?

SID

What does she need? *(They gaze at each other for a moment. SID sighs.)* Me. My life... My story.

ANDY

I got that. But why?

SID

Why indeed?

SONG: KNOCK KNOCK REPRISE

SID (CONT'D)

Knock knock

ANDY

Who's there?

SID

Someone demanding answers
Who's gonna keep on knocking till she gets them

ANDY

Knock knock

SID

Who's there?

ANDY

That girl is like a cancer
Poisoning our peace with her resentment
She stands in your glow
Draws warmth from your sun
So many flock to you for guidance
But not that one

I don't trust her motives, Sidney

SID

She says that I am hiding
Am I?
There's healing in confiding
That is true
Oh who is it that she reminds...

ANDY

Why won't she
Respect your boundaries?
I don't believe
That she is what she seems
Maybe I should just ask her to leave

SID

We cannot turn away one who comes to us in need

ANDY

But since you'll never tell her your life story

SID

I didn't say that.

ANDY

You mean...

After all these years
All these long and silent years
Why?
Why her?

(ANDY exits.)

SONG: FORCE OF NATURE

SID

Noticing the light
Filter through the blinds
Something about her face

Noticing the chill
Creeping up my spine
Another time and place

Noticing the blood
Pounding in my head
An overwhelming draw

Noticing the thrill
Noticing the dread
A frozen stream must thaw
Deep within
Warming
Spidery cracks
Forming

Is it just the moon that turns the tides
And the sun that melts the ice?
There's a force of nature in her eyes
A mighty power

After all these years
Long and silent years
An urge to speak arises

Watch the feeling grow
Ask it what it knows
Open to life's surprises

Thoughts lead to words, and words lead to actions
But silence too Can mean attachment

Is it just the moon that turns the tides
And the sun that melts the ice
There's a force of nature in your eyes
A mighty power

Sid, let go
Oh, don't resist the flow

Now I'm noticing the air
Noticing the fear
Stop holding on now
Be strong now
Let it go

(Raina appears upstage, in shadow)

SID AND RAINA
It isn't just the moon that turns the tides
And the sun that melts the ice
There's a force of nature in your eyes
A mighty power

SID
After all these years
Long and silent years
Now it is time
Now it is time

SCENE 11

SID and RAINA in Sid's yurt.

SID
It's been so long since I've talked about any of this. I
know it's "my" life - I lived it - and yet –

RAINA
Uh huh.

SID
I'm sorry. You were asking about Bois Riche. But as a
child, you see, it seemed completely...ordinary. It was all
I knew.

RAINA
Weren't you curious about the outside world?

SID

As I grew older, yes. Some of my friends traveled and told stories, and I wanted... But my father was adamant that I should stay within the walls and I...I loved him. I didn't want to hurt him.

RAINA

I loved my father and I hurt him all the time.

SID

Loved?

RAINA

(Nods) He's gone. He...died.

SID

Recently?

RAINA

Yeah.

SID

I'm sorry.

RAINA

What about your mother?

SID

Peace-

RAINA

We're not talking about me.

SID

But-

RAINA

Please. Your mother.

SID

(Slight pause.) I never met my mother. She died in childbirth.

RAINA

Oh. *(Slight pause)* Did you miss her?

SID

Oh God, yes. Especially when I was a teenager and my dad had me under a microscope. I used to daydream about this amazing mom. She was like a best friend, only better, because she understood everything I was going through, but she wasn't caught up in it herself.

RAINA

I know what you mean. I never knew my mother either.

SID

Oh?

RAINA

I missed her. I loved her. But I hated her more. I still do.

SID

Did-

RAINA

But we're talking about you, remember? How you were a good girl.

SID

(Nods) I was. A "good girl." I always did what my daddy told me. Didn't drink, didn't smoke, never let boys get too close. I never even told a lie, until...

RAINA

Until?

SID

Until the night the prophecy began to unfold.

SCENE 12

SID and YASHA are scaling the wall around Bois Riche.
They whisper, self-conscious about being overheard.

YASHA
Are you sure you want to do this?

SID
Yes.

YASHA
Because we could just go to the kids' club here in the community-

SID
No.

YASHA
I just don't want you to do something you're gonna regret. If your dad finds out-

SID
He won't.

YASHA
But if he does-

SID
It's my eighteenth birthday, Yasha, and I've never been outside these walls. If I chicken out now, what kind of life am I gonna have?

YASHA
I'm just saying, maybe you should talk to him first, get him to-

SID
If I ask him, he'll say no. And then he'll watch me more closely than ever. He might even recode the alarm or hide some new cameras or something. I know he just

wants to protect me, but I can't live the rest of my life as his little girl. I have to make my own way. If he finds out, then...I'll live with the consequences.

(SID scrambles over the wall. A car horn honks.)

SID (CONT'D)
There's our ride. Come on!

SCENE 13

Lights indicate traffic coming and going. Techno music, sirens, traffic sounds. SID and YASHA have just gotten out of the car in the city and are immediately surrounded by homeless people, who pull them slightly apart.

SONG: THE REAL THING

SLEAZY MAN
Hey lady, sweet lady, hey where you headed to?

DRUNKEN MAN
Hey kiddos, wait kiddos, I think I remember you

RECENTLY UNEMPLOYED MAN
Hey buddy wanna score some crystal?

HOMELESS WOMAN
I just need a place to squat

SCARED WOMAN
My man is raging and he's got a pistol

SLEAZY MAN
Hey girl, you're lookin' hot!
Can I have your number?

RECENTLY UNEMPLOYED MAN
Won't you cut me a break?

HOMELESS WOMAN

I just need a hot meal

SCARED WOMAN

Oh please keep me safe

RECENTLY UNEMPLOYED MAN

Some money for train fare

DRUNKEN MAN

Money for beer

SLEAZY MAN

Can I have your number?

MEN

Just blow in my ear.

ALL

You wanted the real thing
The real thing
The sharp sting
You're craving the hard dark flavor
Of what life is
I'll show you the real thing
The real thing
The real thing
The harsh fling
I'll give you a wake-up smack
And you'll start to live
Just look at me
Just look at me

> *(The crowd parts to reveal DELILAH, a drag queen,*
> *dressed in layers of ragged lace and beads. She looks*
> *emaciated and very sick, with sores in plain view.*
> *The others give her a wide berth. She is lit in a*
> *luminous way, to indicate that she is the first*
> *messenger.)*

DELILAH

Just look at me
In my face you will see
Brutal reality

(DELILAH coughs.)

SID

You're sick.

DELILAH

Yes. And you are?

SID

Sid. Sidney. Sidney Arthur.

DELILAH

Pleasure to meet you, Miss Sid Arthur. I'm Delilah.

Back when I ran this city
They called me "Empress D"
Little girl you're so pretty
You remind me of me
Back when I was a sweet thing
The belle of the ball
Boys and girls, queens, kings
I dazzled them all.

But now you see that my youth has
Been nipped in the bud
By this ruthless intruder
Invading my blood
Devouring my muscles
Consuming my bones
Leaving only the memories
Of all that I've known

SID

Is there anything that I can do for you?

DELILAH

Are you God? If you are, there's a thing or two.
Startin' out with a fat shot of morphine for the pain
Then you can add a clean pair of lungs and
Kindly vanquish the chills and the runs and
While you're at it, can you sharpen up my brain?

(DELILAH collapses in a fit of coughing)

DELILAH (CONT'D)

So are you God?

SID

No, I am not.

DELILAH

Then you can't help
Me or anyone else,
No, not even yourself.

(SID stares. The crowd closes in around her.)

ALL

You wanted the real thing
The real thing
The sharp sting
You're craving the jagged edges of
What life is
Well this is the real thing
The real thing
The deep spring
This is the moment when you
Begin to live

(HAG, an old woman, hobbles onto the stage, carrying bags of groceries.)

HAG

Hag coming through
Hag coming through

Out of my way
Out of my way
Or inhale the bouquet
Of my new pepper spray!

(Homeless people part to reveal SID and YASHA.)

HAG (CONT'D)

Well lookie here.

A coupla freshly minted swells from
Bois Riche, Bois Riche
Bois Riche, Bois Riche

SID

How'd you know?

HAG

Sneaking out while daddy's snoozing
for hanky panky, smokes and boozing

SID

No!

HAG

Now don't play the innocent with me.

(Sid stares.)

HAG (CONT'D)

Just close up that gaping squeak-hole
Don't stare at me like i'm a freak
Or do i divine this is the first time
that you've ever seen an antique?

SID

Of course I've seen old people before.

HAG

Those face-lifted, botoxed fifty-year-olds in Bois Riche?

SID

Some of them are fifty-five, I think.

HAG

Ha!

This jowly face and flabby belly
Breath that reeks of rot and mold
Veiny legs and tits like jelly
This is what it means to be old.

And believe me, it feels as bad as it looks.

Aching back, swollen feet, and a frozen knee
Failing eyes, failing ears, fading memory
Hard to sleep, hard to pee, and libido is a joke

Add to the pain and humiliation
The booby prize for this drawn-out staycation:
Is watching all your friends and family croak.

See what you have to look forward to?

(She exits. Homeless people close in.)

ALL

You ran from your mansion
In search of the real
For one night to slum it
And learn how it feels
To make eyes at danger
To flirt with the knife
To move to the muscular rhythms of life
You came for the real thing
And now that you've found it
You want to escape but
You find you're surrounded
You're starting to feel like
You're under attack
But once you have gone there
There's no turning back

79

(Scene shifts to Bois Riche. SUNNY lies on the floor, a paramedic covering him with a sheet. SID and YASHA enter.)

SID

What...Dad?! What happened?

PARAMEDIC

Heart attack. I'm sorry, Miss. He's dead.

SID

No! Oh no. Oh no. Oh no. Oh no. Oh no.

(The people SID met in the city appear around the periphery, creating a psychological backdrop to the action.)

ALL

You wanted the real thing
The real thing

HAG AND DELILAH

Four messengers

ALL

This is what life is
The real thing
The real thing

HAG AND DELILAH

Four messengers

ALL

This is what life is
This is the path
This is the path
This is the path
And there's no turning back.

END OF ACT 1

Tanya Shaffer and Vienna Teng

ACT 2, SCENE 1

Sid stands center, while the ensemble, dressed in yogi clothes, slowly draws an enormous silk sheet over her. The tone is dirge-like.

SONG: PEBBLE IN A LAKE REPRISE

YOGIS
Every choice that we make
Is a pebble in a lake
Spreading ripples beyond our sight
Every step that we take
Impresses its shape
On a galaxy of lives

Every choice that we make
Is a pebble in a lake
Spreading ripples beyond our sight
Every step that we take
Impresses its shape
On a galaxy of lives

Every choice that we make
Is a pebble in a lake
Spreading ripples beyond our sight
Every step that we take
Impresses its shape
On a galaxy of lives

> *(Lights fade up on high school aged SID lying in her bed, curled in a fetal position. YASHA sits on the bed. She faces away from him.)*

YASHA
Come on, Sid-Sid. It'll be fun.

SID
You go ahead.

YASHA

Ashley's dad just put in a wave pool.

SID

Sounds cool.

YASHA

So come check it out.

SID

Why?

YASHA

Because. You can't lie here forever. I know you're sad about your dad, but it's been three months. You've gotta get on with your life. (Delicately) Have you thought of talking to a...a counselor or something?

SID

Why? So they can slam the rosy blinders back on? Convince me I didn't see what I saw, that I don't know what I know?

YASHA

Sidney, listen –

SID

No, you listen.

Everything that we've known
Everything we call our own
Is a hollow and pompous lie
From the moment of our birth
We're taught we rule the earth
And that we will never die
why play along with that illusion
When everything we love we are born to lose
What is the point?

YASHA

Look to your friends, let us care for you
We're here to lend an ear and a shoulder
You can depend on what is right in front of you
Walk through this open door
Lay down your burdens for a while

SID

Everything that we feel
Everything we think is real
Is elusive as rising steam
Everything that we build
Is a promise unfulfilled
No more solid than a dream
What is the point of moving forward
Our fate is set no matter which road we choose
What is the point?

YASHA

I was beside you, I saw it all too
I realize there's no easy answer
Look in my eyes, I'll tell you what I know is true
This much I'm certain of
Maybe it's not enough
But Sidney-I love you
I always have
And I always will

SID

Everything that we've known

YASHA

You don't have to feel alone
When you think of what you saw that night

SID

Everything that we feel

YASHA

You can trust that this is real
Come let me hold you tight

SID

When I feel your arms around me
I can believe

BOTH

We'll be alright somehow

YASHA

Let my love shelter you

SID

Yasha, I love you too

BOTH

Maybe this is all we need for now.

> *(Lights shift, so that YASHA and SID are in shadow
> or silhouette. While the yogis sing, YASHA and SID
> slowly undress and begin making love.)*

YOGIS

Every choice that we make
Is a pebble in a lake
Spreading ripples beyond our sight
with every step that we take
Let the choices we make
Bring us closer to the light

So let me look to the thought
For thoughts lead to words
Look to the words
For words lead to actions
Look to the action
For actions lead to habits
Habit leads to character
Character becomes destiny.

SCENE 2

*Raina in the office, on the phone. Sam at his desk. Raina
speaks continuously over Sam's first two interjections.*

SAM

Messengers.

RAINA

Right. Like in the prophecy. The drag queen was sickness, the old woman was aging -

SAM

Sweetie-

RAINA

- and her father was death, but-

SAM

Sweetheart -

RAINA

- no one seems to have any idea who the fourth messenger was. Which is strange because -

SAM

Raina!

RAINA

Yeah?

SAM

This is about as newsworthy as my mom's new haircut.

RAINA

This is just backstory –

SAM

Backstory for what? Sex, drugs, money? What's our angle here?

RAINA

(Slight pause) I can't say yet.

SAM

Why not? The Raina I know would've had a complete draft to me by now. Hell, she would've had it days ago. Look, if there's no story, let's cut our losses and get you home. It happens.

RAINA

There is a story. I told you. I just –

SAM

"Can't say yet." *(Slight pause)* Prophecies and messengers...You're not going native on me, are you?

RAINA

"Going native"?

SAM

Becoming one of them? Woo-woo, meditation, chanting, gonna come back as a holy cow?

RAINA

That's Hindu.

SAM

Okay, an elephant.

RAINA

Sammy!

SAM

I'm just asking: are you becoming emotionally involved?

RAINA

No!

SAM

Because you know that's a bad idea.

RAINA

I thought you wanted me more "emotionally available."

SAM

To me! Not to some goddamn guru. This is work, Raina, not -

RAINA

And work and emotion should never mix.

SAM

Damn right! Wait, what are we talking about here?

RAINA

I need more time.

SAM

(Overlapping) No way.

RAINA

There's a lot of...layers...to get through...

SAM

Seriously? You're giving me nothing but fairy tales, and now you want me to okay, what, another two-three days-

RAINA

A week.

SAM

What a comedian.

RAINA

Come on.

SAM

I admire your persistence, babe, but I've got a publisher to answer to, a staff asking questions... I can't keep throwing money at smoke!

RAINA

Don't pay me.

SAM

Raina-

RAINA

I mean it.

SAM

(Sighs) Fine. Two. More. Days.

SCENE 3

DEREKH, MIKE, and MYRA cross the stage, pushing
brooms.

DEREKH

General studies! I found it in the catalogue last night.

MIKE

What the hell kind of major is that?

MYRA

Language...

DEREKH

You take fifteen credits per semester of whatever
subjects you want. It's like majoring in everything. It's
perfect!

(Lights shift to RAINA and SID, in SID's yurt.)

SID

Andy and I went from one community, one practice, one
teacher to another. But after years of that, I still hadn't
found what I was looking for. I needed to strip it all
away and start from scratch. So I said goodbye to Andy,
and I told him that if I ever found what I was looking
for, I'd come back and share it with him. Then I took a
vow of silence. And for seven years, I walked the earth.

RAINA

Homeless?

SID

Houseless, was how I thought of it.

RAINA

And in all that time, you didn't say a word?

SID

No. After a while, I practically forgot I'd ever spoken at all. Instead, I listened.

RAINA

To what?

SID

Everything. Birds. Insects. Cats. Wolves. *(RAINA looks surprised.)* I could hear them in the mountains outside of town when the moon was full... Engines starting, turning over, dying. Human voices calling out greetings, songs, exclamations of joy and frustration, laughter and pain. The sounds of things meeting, rubbing, slapping against each other: metal on metal, water on earth, skin on skin. And behind the sound, silence, like a bottomless pool. And all of us living beings were just insects skating on that silence, never even piercing the surface.

I'd tried so hard to understand the nature of suffering, when all I really wanted was to dissolve into that stillness.

So I sat down.

(Lights and set shift to reveal the freeway overpass. SID sits under it.)

SONG: I WILL NOT RISE

SID (CONT'D)

And put an end to all my wandering
And put an end to striving to learn the truth

I've had enough, I'll go no farther
And from this moment on I will not be moved
I will sit calm and firm as a mountain
Clear as empty air
Open as sky
Until I touch
What doesn't die
I will not eat
I will not sleep
I will not rise

> *(Traffic noises resume. People appear and disappear*
> *on different parts of the stage, noticing Sid, their*
> *voices overlapping, perhaps distorted.)*

SID

In, out, in, out.

For several days, people came and went. Then the real
circus began.

(POLICE OFFICER 1 enters, talking on his radio. IN, OUT
underscoring continues.)

POLICE OFFICER 1

10-4. Checking out a complaint about a lady sitting
under the I-90 overpass.... Hup, and here she is.
(Approaches SID.) Ummm, lady, there's no loitering here.
City ordinance number 23786.

> *(SID does not respond.)*

POLICE OFFICER 1 (CONT'D)

Lady? I said you're gonna have to move. There's a
shelter just up the road if you need a place to stay.
(Pause) Aww, lady. Why you gotta make it hard on
yourself? *(Pause)* Awright, here we go. You're under
arrest for loitering; you have the right to remain silent–
(Tries to lift her) Jesus, lady, you're heavier'n you look.
(Tries again several times, grunting and straining.) Jesus

Christ almighty. *(Talks into his radio.)* I'm gonna need some backup.

> *(POLICE OFFICER exits, then re-enters, accompanied by several other POLICE OFFICERS.)*

POLICE OFFICERS

10-4.

> *(Together, the POLICE OFFICERS try to move SID, but are unable to budge her. They exit, shaking their heads. A few moments later, POLICE OFFICER 1 comes back, directing a bulldozer. The bulldozer attempts to move SID, but is unable to do so. It drives away. POLICE OFFICER follows, gesticulating.)*

REPORTER

I'm reporting live from the site of the silent lady dubbed "Freeway Frieda," whom the entire city police department has apparently been unable to move. Her presence has become something of a touchstone for homeless rights activists...

PROTESTERS

Hell no, she won't go!
Hell no, she won't go!

SID

Eventually, they lost interest and went away.

> *(POLICE OFFICERS and PROTESTERS throw up their hands and leave.)*

SID (CONT'D)

My next challenge came from a lot closer to home.

> *(A rumbling sound is heard.)*

TUMMY

Sidney! This is your tummy calling. *(Pause)* Sidney!
Answer me!

SID

In, out...

TUMMY

Feed me...

SID

Shh! Go away!

TUMMY

You can't talk to me like that. I've got friends, you know.

SID

I said hush!

TUMMY

Fine. *(Crackling sound, as of radio.)* I'm gonna need some
backup.

> *(A loaf of BREAD enters. SID sniffs, groans
> longingly.)*

SID

Oooh, what's that smell?

SONG: SID'S TEMPTATIONS, PART 1: BREAD AND WATER

BREAD

Comin' fresh from the oven
I'm golden and hot
Give your taste buds some lovin'
Yeah I'll hit the spot
The aroma's rising
Rich and surprising
Yum yum yum yum, aaaaaaah!

CHORUS

Yum yum yum yum, aaaaaaah!

BREAD

Slather me with butter, baby
Spread me with a sweet red jam
Ooh baby don't you know who I am?

SID

Bread…

CHORUS

Bread!

SID

I'm hungry…

CHORUS

So hungry

SID

And thirsty too...

(A glass of WATER runs on.)

WATER

Oo, that's my cue!

You're a scorching desert inside
Every inch of you crumbled and dry
I can heal you, I can provide
This cool, cool water

CHORUS

Cool, cool water

WATER

It's easy, I'm here for you
Pour this glorious river right into you

WATER AND CHORUS
Glug glug glug glug glug glug
Glug glug glug glug glug glug aaaaah!

SID
(With difficulty) Go away. Mine is a thirst you cannot soothe.

(BREAD and WATER approach ominously.)

WATER AND CHORUS
Glug glug glug glug glug glug
Glug glug glug glug glug glug

BREAD AND CHORUS
Yum yum yum yum yum yum
Yum yum yum yum-

SID
I said shoo! I have a job to do.

(WATER and BREAD exit in disgust.)

RAINA
So how long...

SID
I don't know. I lost track of time. Then I entered a whole other realm.

(MAY appears as an ANGEL, joined by other ANGELS.)

**SONG: SID'S TEMPTATIONS, PART 2:
SLEEP/HUNDRED THOUSAND LIFETIMES**

MAY AND ANGELS
Sleep, sleep
Sleep, sleep

MAY
Poor sweetheart. You're exhausted.

SID

Mama?

MAY

Who else?

SID

Oh, Mama. I've missed you so. All my life.

MAY

Then join me.

SID

Right now?

MAY

Of course.

SID

(Rousing slightly) But...you're dead.

MAY

Exactly. It's so peaceful! Isn't that what you want: to be at peace?

SID

But my work here's not done.

MAY

You'll finish it some other time.

There are many lifetimes to be lived
May and angels
Maybe next time you'll have more to give
Now sleep, sleep

What's one little lifetime, anyway?

(RAINA steps into the scene)

RAINA

Your mother?

SID

Yes.

RAINA

Didn't you want to stay with her?

SID

Oh, I did. But when she said...

MAY

What's one little lifetime, anyway?

SID

It was like a door opened inside me...

(As SID sings the following, the ensemble enters and stands behind May, a sea of faces stretching back.)

SID (CONT'D)

And suddenly I see
Stretched out behind me
The bodies I have occupied
The people I have loved
The tears I have cried
The deaths I have died
A hundred thousand lifetimes
Searching, searching
A hundred thousand lifetimes Is enough
This time I'll see it through
It's what I have to do

MAY AND ENSEMBLE

You break my heart.

SID

I know it.
I break my own heart too.

97

RAINA

And then... Was that the moment? Your final-

SID

Oh no. Not yet. Not at all.

(Sound of rain. Lights indicate nightfall, a storm. YASHA enters, eerily lit, exactly as he was in high school)

SONG, SID'S TEMPTATIONS, PART 5: COME BACK TO ME

YASHA

Sidney.

SID

Yasha!

RAINA

(From the sidelines) Oh.

YASHA

My Sidney, why'd you run away?
I've been aching for you night and day,
Day and night, with all my soul

SID

Oh, Yasha, I didn't mean to hurt you...

YASHA

Why won't you let me wrap my arms around you
And feel your troubles melt into the ground
I'll make everything right; I'll make you whole

SID

Yasha, I miss you!

YASHA

Then come back to me

(Ensemble joins in, singing "ah" and "mm" in the background.)

YASHA (CONT'D)

Come back to me
I've learned so much, I'm no longer a boy – You'll see!
I'll kiss you where you're sore
Don't suffer anymore
Come back to me, there's much to enjoy

SID

Oh, I would like that...

Oh Yasha, how I miss the heat
That electric tingle, sharp and sweet
Pressed against you in the dark
Delicious urgency in every move
Maybe this is the only kind of truth
Skin on skin

SID & YASHA

Heart to heart
So come back to me

ENSEMBLE

It's not too late for

SID & YASHA

Come back to me

ENSEMBLE

What we're made for

SID & YASHA

I/You have wandered so long, now it's time to come home

ENSEMBLE

Sweet home

YASHA

All is forgiven

ENSEMBLE

And more

SID

The moment I walk in

CHORUS

That door

YASHA

So come back

CHORUS

Ah

YASHA

Come back

SID & CHORUS

Ah

YASHA

Come back

SID & CHORUS

Ah

YASHA

Come back to me...

SID & CHORUS
Oh yes, oh yes, oh yes, oh yes, oh yes, oh yes, oh–
SID
No! (Music drops out. More softly) I can't. Go away,
Yasha.

(Yasha backs away, a terrible sadness on his face.)

RAINA

How could you do that?

SID

What?

RAINA

How could you reject him like that? He was just a kid.

SID

He wasn't real. I had to release all-

RAINA

Nothing's real to you, is it? Nothing ever was. He never got over you. He made me promise not to go after you. So I didn't. Not while he was alive.

SID

He-

RAINA

Oh, God, I miss him. I miss him so much.

(RAINA sobs uncontrollably. SID moves toward her.)

RAINA (CONT'D)

Leave me alone!

(She runs offstage. YOGIS disperse silently. They were never really there. SID looks after RAINA, stunned, as the realization suddenly dawns are her.)

SID

Raina!

(She runs out after RAINA.)

SCENE 4

*The snowy field behind the meditation hall. RAINA runs out,
heading away from the buildings, toward the woods. SID
comes out after her.*

SID

Raina.

RAINA

Leave me alone!

SID

Raina, where are you going?

(SID grabs her, puts the blanket around her.)

RAINA

Take your hands off me! Why are you saying my name?
You don't know me!

SID

Come back. There's nothing but woods out here. You'll
freeze.

RAINA

What the hell do you care? All these years, you've never
cared.

SID

Raina –

RAINA

Why did you do it?

SID

What?

RAINA

Why did you leave me?

SID

Let's go inside.

RAINA

No. Here.

SID

You're shivering. We'll-

RAINA

Tell me!

SID

Okay... *(Breath)* I... Well... After my father died, I lost...
Everything went blank... But then, being with Yasha -
your dad - for a while it, I closed my eyes. For a while,
I... I let myself forget.

RAINA

Forget what?

SID

What I'd seen. What I knew. But then...

RAINA

Then?

SID

Then...you. You looked at me with that steady gaze, so
open, so trusting, so utterly unadorned.

SONG: FORCE OF NATURE REPRISE

SID (CONT'D)

I feel my world expand
And now I understand
You are every child on earth
Every child is you
i see we're one now
And somehow
I must raise us all

And that is when I know
I know I have to go

RAINA

I don't understand.

SID

The fourth messenger
The fourth messenger
It was you
Oh, It was you.

RAINA

I was a messenger?

SID

Yes.

RAINA

So it's my fault you left?

SID

Fault? No! You inspired me. You gave me the courage to find another way.

RAINA

Oh my God.

SID

We're not separate, Raina, not really. In this relative realm, yes, we have these separate bodies, separate stories, but in the absolute–

RAINA

Wait a minute, what? This isn't some abstract... You fucked someone. You brought a child into this world, and you didn't take responsibility for it! Where were you when I needed you? When I was sick, when I was lonely, when I had to ask my father to buy me my first bra, all the millions of times I needed a mother?

SONG: WHAT ABOUT ME?

RAINA (CONT'D)
Every time I'd see your face
Flash across a TV screen
Every time your name appeared
In another glossy magazine
Every time I'd hear you quoted
Every time I'd hear you praised
By some student so devoted,
Somebody whose life you saved,
Every time I'd hear a stranger
Rave about how much you give
How you walk divine among us
How you show us how to live
I'd want to rage
I'd want to cry
I'd want to tell them it's all a lie
I'd want to howl up to the sky:
What about me?
What about me?
How can it be
This miraculous "she"
Could forget about me?

SID
(Tries to take her hand) Raina.

RAINA
No!

Every time I'd see a woman
Lift a baby to her breast
Walk a toddler 'cross the street
Or Scold a teen on how she's dressed
Every time I read about
How every mother loves her child
In my mouth the taste grows bitter
In my chest my heart beats wild
Every time I think of how

105

You left me when I had no voice
No words to tell you how I need you
No power that could sway your choice
I want to rage
I want to cry
I want to tell them it's all a lie
I want to howl up to the sky:
What about me?
What about me?
How can it be
This miraculous "she"
Could forget about me?

To sit there in the room with you
Hear your laughter, see your smile
It's not as i imagined it would be
My heart's a knot, a book shut tight
Unreadable even to me
every time you meet my eyes
I lose my tether, lose my drive
Why do they love you?
Why can't I hate you?
Oh why don't you know that I'm alive
How can it be
This miraculous she

The teacher, the prophet, the seer, the sage
The one who shines light on this desolate age
The one whose compassion is vaster than earth
Who shows us the cycle of death and rebirth...
Oh how is it true
This miraculous you
Could just walk away
Stray till today
From your own body's issue
Your sinew, your tissue
This stubborn but vulnerable
Still, I hope, lovable
Me?

SID

I'm sorry, Raina. I'm sorry.

RAINA

Are you? Are you sorry you left?

SID

I'm sorry for your suffering.

RAINA

But you're not sorry you left.

SID

(Breath) No. *(Pause.)* I left because the task before me demanded everything I had: all my concentration, all my focus, all my love. I'd seen the face of suffering and the possibility of release from that suffering, and I couldn't turn away.

RAINA

So you turned away from me instead.

SID

Yes.

RAINA

And you never looked back.

SID

(With feeling) Oh, but I did. I carried you with me, for years.

SCENE 5

A dark stage. A crib. As SID sings, members of the company becomes SID, one by one enacting the different moments of her life. They dress in identical garments, probably the ones she wore during the first "You've Got a Glow" and/or when sitting under the freeway.

SONG: YOU ARE THERE

SID

This is the part where I kiss your head
You're sleeping soundly; I don't want to wake you
This is the part where I pack my bag
I pack light, I can't afford to take too much...
This is the part where I fold up the note
That I wrote to Yasha, I prop it on the table,
This is the part where I stop at the door,
Drop my bag and run to kiss your head ONCE MORE...
This is the part where tears come
This is the part where I turn to run
This is the part where I double over
The pain is overwhelming as the day you were born

This is the part where I split in two
Strange as it sounds, there's no other way to say it
One of me turns, but the other scoops you up,
And you're so light, you don't weigh a thing...
That's how I bring you with me

And everywhere I go
You are always there
A thousand miles from home
You are always there
We gaze at the planets,
Sleep on a park bench,
Wake to a flashlight's glare,
You are there.
You are always there.
Scavenging to eat
You are always there
I sing you to sleep
A lullaby prayer
And you give me strength
To keep on searching
Year after wandering year
A reason to care
You are there

RAINA

Was I there?

SID

You were there

RAINA

Was I always there?

SID

You were always there

SID AND RAINA

In this life we share

RAINA

I am always there

SID

You are always...

> *(SID positions herself beneath the freeway, exactly as she was during the temptations sequence.)*

SID (CONT'D)

This is the part where I face the truth
Admit to myself that I left you long ago

RAINA

No...

SID

The part where all illusions die

RAINA

Don't leave me, Mama

SID

This is the moment I leave behind
All that I knew

RAINA

Oh Mama, No

SID

All that I was

RAINA

Mama, no

SID

All that I held
All that I loved
Goodbye
This is the moment I am no longer "I"...

> *(An earth-shaking rumble starts, low at first, then building. As RAINA watches helplessly from the edge of the stage, SID's breathing becomes louder. On the scrim her shadow grows larger and larger until it is enormous. The music rises and rises. SID reaches out her hand and touches the earth. She speaks in a voice unlike any she has used before.)*

SID (CONT'D)

As the earth bears witness to the work I've done over a hundred thousand lifetimes, I have the right to be free.

> *(There is a brilliant flash, and the stage goes dark. Lights creep slowly back up.)*

RAINA

So...what...what happened? Did you...

SID

Emptiness. I was nothing, and I was everything. No separation. And I was at peace. Finally.*(Pause. Emphatically)* Raina.

RAINA

Yes?

SID

Thank you.

RAINA

For what?

SID

For coming here and... breaking it all apart. I always told
myself that I didn't discuss my past because it would
distract people from the teachings. But now I see it was
never about them. It was me. I was afraid of what it
would do to me to re-open that part of myself. Even
after all I'd learned, I couldn't face the memory of you.
So I put it away.

RAINA

Oh.

SID

But now...there's something here, Raina, something I feel
when I'm with you, that...it's different. It's more than I
could have imagined.

There's love for all beings, and then there's...there's this.
There's you. You and me. I don't understand it, but I'd
love to explore it more deeply.

Will you stay a while, and teach me?

RAINA

(Taken aback) I...I don't know.

SCENE 6

*MIKE and MYRA are talking outside the dining hall.
REPORTER 1 enters, wearing a parka and rolling a small
suitcase.*

MYRA

It's all lies! Why are they persecuting her?

MIKE

Here comes another one.

REPORTER 1

Nell Wyatt, Juice Magazine. Any idea where I could find Mama Sid?

MYRA

(Shrieks) Get out of here!

> *(REPORTER 1 exits, rolling his eyes. DEREKH enters.)*

DEREKH

Oh man! She just took off!

MYRA

(Panicked) Mama Sid?

DEREKH

No, Harmony! She, like, flipped out, and caught a ride outta here with some delivery guy!

> *(RAINA enters.)*

RAINA

What's going on?

DEREKH

You tell us.

RAINA

I don't know.

MYRA

Oh you don't, huh? You have no idea why this place is crawling with reporters?

RAINA

No.

DEREKH

You lied to us, Peace.

MIKE

Or whatever your name is.

DEREKH

Why'd you lie?

RAINA

I-

MYRA

(To RAINA) You're not the only one in pain, you know. *(Sobs)*

(Reporter 2 crosses back, tapping on a phone.)

REPORTER 2

(English accent) Hello? Hello? Bloody hell! Know where I could find a loo around here?

(MIKE points.)

DEREKH

Man, this place is nuts.

(DEREKH exits.)

MIKE

(Puts a tentative arm around MYRA, who's still sobbing. He starts steering her off.) Shhhh...You'll tire yourself out.

MYRA

What do you care? You and your "messy attachments."

MIKE

I care.

MYRA

You do?

> *(They exit together. RAINA stares at them, then runs off in the direction of the office.)*

SCENE 7

Sid's yurt. ANDY and SID stand facing each other.

SID

I should have told you.

ANDY

But you didn't trust- You thought I couldn't handle it.

SID

I couldn't handle it. You, of course I... You're my best friend. I depend on you.

SONG: YOU'VE GOT A GLOW REPRISE

ANDY

So many years
I walked by your side
In awe of the miracle
That brought you to be my guide
My unearthly angel
My beacon of truth
And as you depend on me
I depended on you

My life's direction and course
I gave over in service to yours
But there is so much you concealed
That I no longer know what is real

You taught me the pain of clinging
And yet I held on
To an image of you that is finally gone
I'm empty inside
But now I know
Sidney, dear Sidney,
I have to go.

> *(ANDY exits. SID watches him leave, fighting back tears, as the music swells.)*

SID
(Whispers) Goodbye, Andy.

SCENE 8

RAINA is in the office, on the phone.

SAM (V.O.)
This is Debunk Nation editor-in-chief Sam Skara –

> *(Sam enters. RAINA's back is to him.)*

SAM (V.O.)
Please leave your message at the tone.

> *(Sam comes up behind her and puts his arms around her.)*

SAM
(Murmuring) Please leave your message at the tone.

RAINA
(Overlapping) Sam!

> *(He kisses her.)*

RAINA (CONT'D)
What are you doing here?

SONG: THE TRUTH MUST COME OUT REPRISE

SAM

I hopped a plane
I brought champagne
To toast your big success
We ran your story this morning
I give you fair warning
It's bigger than we could've guessed
Talk show hosts, publishers, producers, agents
They all want to get to you
Baby, you pulled off a coup

You broke the next big story!
The web is ablaze
The next big story
Yeah, it's The next big story
Don't look so amazed
The next big story!

RAINA

But I didn't file –

SAM

You dropped enough hints. Pretty sexy how you strung
me along...

What we ran was just a tease
For your first-person series
"Confessions of a daughter scorned"
You'll be famous and rich;
That hypocritical bitch
Will wish that she was never born!

RAINA

That's not what I want!

SAM

No?

RAINA

How could you betray me like this?

SAM

Betray you? I *launched* you!

RAINA

You should've told me-

SAM

You stopped picking up!

RAINA

You should've waited-

SAM

And let someone else scoop me? *(Pause)* Oh Raina. I
warned you not to get emotionally involved.

RAINA

She's my mother.

SAM

The mother who cast off
Both you and your dad
The one who pretended
That she never had you
You've waited to long to call her to account
And this will make your name
Your breakout story is now her shame
For the truth, yes, the truth must come out.

RAINA

Truth is complicated.

SAM

That's what the liars always say.

RAINA

Is that really all you see?

SAM
I see what's in front of me. And right now that's a kickass, take-no-prisoners little reporter who uses everything at her disposal - and I do mean everything - to get what she wants.

RAINA
I never (used you)-

SAM
Don't apologize. It's what I love about you.

RAINA
And your wife? Does she love that about me too?

SAM
Come on, Raina. You know that's –

RAINA
Complicated?

SAM
Listen.

RAINA
No.

SAM
No what?

RAINA
This isn't who I want to be any more.

SAM
Meaning...?

RAINA
Leave, Sam.

SCENE 9

The meditation hall. Music starts immediately in the blackout. SID stands at the front of the room, reporters and yogis gathered before her.

SONG: AREN'T YOU ASHAMED?

REPORTERS
Mama Sid, Mama Sid, would you give us a statement?

YOGIS
Mama Sid, Mama Sid, are they telling the truth?

REPORTERS
Mama Sid, Mama Sid, does your own daughter hate you?

YOGIS
Mama Sid, Mama Sid, I am really confused.

REPORTERS
Mama Sid, Mama Sid, do you have other secrets?

YOGIS
Mama Sid, Mama Sid, is this some kind of test?

REPORTERS
Mama Sid, Mama Sid, do you prey on their weakness?

(Indicating yogis)

DEREKH, MYRA
Mama Sid, Mama Sid, just don't talk to the press!

REPORTER 1
Mama Sid, will you quit teaching
Now that your past has been exposed?

MYRA AND DEREKH

No!

REPORTER 2

Mama Sid, how can you justify
Being so hard, so brutal, so cold

MYRA

This is totally unfair!

DEREKH

If she were a man, nobody would care!

REPORTER 3

She left her boyfriend alone with an infant

REPORTERS

Never told anyone that she had a kid

MIKE

We thought you'd achieved earthly perfection!

(*The following YOGIS' and REPORTERS' lines are
sung simultaneously.*)

REPORTERS

Aren't you ashamed of what you did?
Aren't you ashamed of what you did?
Aren't you ashamed of what you did, what you did?

YOGIS

Mama Sid, Mama Sid
Mama Sid, Mama Sid
What you did, what you did

ALL

Are you ashamed?

SID

Friends, I am sorry. I was wrong to keep my daughter a
secret all these years. I should have embraced her long
ago.

(SID smiles. Long Pause.)

REPORTER 1
Is that all she's gonna say?

REPORTER 2
That's not much of an apology.
SAM
Have you no shame?

SID
I don't believe in shame. I believe in awakening.

(All clamor at once. The next three lines overlap almost completely. Then MIKE's line jumps out above the others.)

REPORTER 3
Aren't you going to apologize for abandoning her?

REPORTER 1
What about her father? You abandoned him too!

REPORTER 2
What kind of a message does that send your followers?

SAM
What kind of message does that send other dead-beat parents?

MIKE
You owe us an explanation!

RAINA
She's a person. That's the explanation.

(Reporters turn to RAINA. The following lines overlap substantially.)

REPORTER 1

How did it feel to finally meet your mother?

MYRA
(To REPORTERS) Why don't you go home?

REPORTER 2
Raina! Will you write a memoir?

DEREKH
(To REPORTERS) Let them work it out themselves!

REPORTER 3
Does this have anything to do your father's death?

REPORTER 1
Tell us your story!

> *(Reporters all clamor "Tell us your story! Tell us your story!")*

SONG: THIS STORY IS MINE FINAL REPRISE

RAINA
This story was supposed to be
A saga of revenge
I'd sweep in on my righteous steed
And that would be the end
I'd ruin your name
Witness your shame
And then flee
Finally free

Now look at this spectacle:
Hyenas swarming round
They clamor for humiliation
But still you stand your ground
They hunger for blood
But you give back... love

This story
This story

This story
Is not what I planned for...

If my opponent isn't mortified, then where's my victory?
And even if you were ashamed,
What good would it do me?
If I can't drag you back
And make you the mother I always wanted
The mother I thought I needed
The mother you will never be...
And yet you say

SID

Please stay

RAINA

You want me to stay

SID

I want you to stay

RAINA

But how can I stay
When I still don't understand
How your love for me
And your love for all the world
Go hand in hand
What can I be to you?

SID

I want to find out too
What kind of family

RAINA AND SID

We can be

DEREKH

Wait - dude - Mama Sid, if you're so...like...human, does
that mean your breakthrough wasn't real?

SID

Oh, my dear friend... It was as real and vivid and fleeting as every other moment of our lives. Do I carry its wisdom and lightness within me? Always. Does it mean that I'm perfect? Of course not.

SONG: AS LONG AS I AM LIVING

SID (CONT'D)
As long as I am living
There are places yet to go
As long as I am human
I still have the chance to grow
the river forks, each time it bends
I am upended in the flow
And I go on...
I go on...

SID AND RAINA
As long as I am living

RAINA
I can always be surprised

SID AND RAINA
As long as I am human

SID
My ideas can be revised

SID AND RAINA
Our hearts can always break again
No matter how we try to hide
And we go on

SID, RAINA, YOGIS
As long as we are living
The path will twist and wind
As long as we are human
We will stumble as we climb
The more we live, the more we see
How deeply we're entwined

SID AND RAINA

And we go on...

YOGIS

Feel the joy
Feel the grief
The act of naming brings relief

SID AND RAINA

And we go on

YOGIS

Heavy, light, shallow, deep

SID AND RAINA

And on
And we go

SID, RAINA, YOGIS

On in the human experience

REPORTERS

This story

SID, RAINA, YOGIS

We go on in the human experience

REPORTERS

This story

SID, RAINA

As long as we are building

YOGIS

We are loving

REPORTERS

The truth...

SID, RAINA

As long as we are changing

YOGIS

We are laughing

REPORTERS

The truth...

SID, RAINA

As long as we are choosing

YOGIS

We are crying

REPORTERS

The truth...

SID, RAINA

As long as we are human

YOGIS

We are dying

SID, RAINA

As long as we are living

YOGIS

We are living

REPORTERS

The truth...

SID, YOGIS

We are

ALL

Living the human experience.

END OF PLAY

CURTAIN CALL MUSIC
SONG: LOOK TO THE THOUGHT REPRISE

SID

So let us look to the thought

ALL

For thoughts lead to words

SID AND RAINA

Look to the word

ALL

For words lead to actions
Look to the action
For actions lead to habits
Habits lead to character
And character becomes destiny
So may our thoughts be clear
May our words be kind
Our actions skillful
Our habits wise
Character be true
Destinies joyful

SID

For from the tiny seed of thought
The thicket of existence grows

ALL

From the tiny seed of thought
All existence grows
All existence, all existence, all existence
All existence grows.

THANK YOU

We are tremendously grateful to all the individuals and organizations who contributed funds throughout the development of this project. Your generosity makes everything possible. Many thanks as well to the countless members of the Bay Area arts community who have so graciously given their time, talent, insight, and resources to this project, including, but not limited to: Amy Mueller and Playwrights Foundation; Robert Kelley, Leslie Martinson, and TheatreWorks; Kent Nicholson; Patrick Dooley and Shotgun Players; M. Graham Smith; Nancy Carlin; Ira Marlowe; Cheshire Isaacs; Raz Kennedy; Mick Berry; Eryn Allen; Michael Gene Sullivan; Molly Bell; and Brad Dollar and Zoo Labs. Thank you as well to Matt August; to the wonderful teachers of Spirit Rock Meditation Center, especially James Baraz, for your wisdom and kindness, and for your enthusiastic support of our project. Tanya would also like to thank Daniel and Elon, for tolerating the extreme preoccupation of their mama; Bette Ingraham *(presente!)* for her loving care of them; and David Green, Juliet Shaffer, Len Shaffer, Ron and Mary Frances Shaffer, Harry Shaffer *(presente!),* Elena Felder, and the members of the Isabelle Maynard Celebratory Writing Group (Jean Schiffman, Leslie Kirk Campbell, and Turi Ryder) for years of moral/emotional/creative support.

TANYA SHAFFER's (PLAYWRIGHT/LYRICIST)
plays have been produced by Berkeley Repertory
Theatre, San Diego Repertory Theatre, A Contemporary
Theatre, TheatreWorks, and the Eureka Theatre, and
have toured to over 40 cities nationwide. She has co-
written two shows for the Tony-Award-Winning San
Francisco Mime Troupe, including 2014's *Ripple Effect*.
Her solo show *Let My Enemy Live Long!* ran for six sold-
out months in the Bay Area and won a Bay Area Theatre
Critics Circle Award. Her play *Baby Taj* was selected by
the San Francisco Chronicle, the San Jose Mercury News,
and the Oakland Tribune as one of the Top Ten Shows of
the Year and was published by Samuel French, Inc. She's
also the author of the acclaimed travel memoir,
Somebody's Heart is Burning: A Woman Wanderer in Africa.
Her stories have appeared on salon.com and in
numerous anthologies. www.tanyashaffer.com

VIENNA TENG's (COMPOSER/CO-LYRICIST)
sixth album, AIMS, received four Independent Music
Awards – for Adult Contemporary Album, Pop Song, A
Cappella Song, and Social Action Song – the most
awards any artist has received in a given year. AIMS
debuted at #4 on Billboard's Heartseekers Albums Chart
and was included in the Best of 2013 lists of the
Huffington Post, NJ Star-Ledger, and Glide Magazine.
She has appeared on The Late Show with David
Letterman, NPR's Weekend Edition, CBS's Early Show,
and CNN's News Night with Aaron Brown, and has
toured with Joan Baez, Brandi Carlile, Duncan Sheik,
Madeleine Peyroux, Joan Osborne, Sarah Harmer, Marc
Cohn and the Indigo Girls, among others. In addition to
her performing and composing career, Vienna recently
received an MB/MS from the Erb Institute for Global
Sustainable Enterprise at the University of Michigan,
and holds a Computer Science degree from Stanford
University. www.viennateng.com

www.thefourthmessenger.com
info@thefourthmessenger.com

CPSIA information can be obtained
at www.ICGtesting.com
Printed in the USA
FSOW01n0018021115
12813FS